Close-Up

# What is a liquid?

by Lynn Peppas

🌱 Crabtree Publishing Company

www.crabtreebooks.com

**Author**
Lynn Peppas

**Publishing plan research and development**
Sean Charlebois, Reagan Miller
Crabtree Publishing Company

**Editor**
Kathy Middleton

**Proofreader**
Wendy Scavuzzo

**Photo research and graphic design**
Katherine Berti

**Print and production coordinator**
Katherine Berti

**Photographs**
Thinkstock: pages 8, 9 (bottom left)
Other images by Shutterstock

**Library and Archives Canada Cataloguing in Publication**

Peppas, Lynn
    What is a liquid? / Lynn Peppas.

(Matter close-up)
Includes index.
Issued also in electronic format.
ISBN 978-0-7787-0770-7 (bound).--ISBN 978-0-7787-0777-6 (pbk.)

    1. Liquids--Juvenile literature.  I. Title.  II. Series: Matter close-up

QC145.24.P47 2012        j530.4'2        C2012-903941-1

**Library of Congress Cataloging-in-Publication Data**

CIP available at Library of Congress

# Crabtree Publishing Company

www.crabtreebooks.com        1-800-387-7650

Printed in Hong Kong/092012/BK20120629

**Published in Canada**
**Crabtree Publishing**
616 Welland Ave.
St. Catharines, Ontario
L2M 5V6

**Published in the United States**
**Crabtree Publishing**
PMB 59051
350 Fifth Avenue, 59th Floor
New York, New York 10118

**Published in the United Kingdom**
**Crabtree Publishing**
Maritime House
Basin Road North, Hove
BN41 1WR

**Published in Australia**
**Crabtree Publishing**
3 Charles Street
Coburg North
VIC 3058

# Contents

# Liquid matters

**Matter** is all around us. We walk on it, swim in it, and breathe it in. Matter is anything that takes up space. Matter has **mass**. Mass is the amount of **particles**, or material, in an object. Matter is made up of billions of tiny particles that are so small we cannot see them with our eyes.

There are three main **states**, or forms, of matter: liquid, solid, and gas. This book is about liquid matter. Liquid is matter that moves. Orange juice, milk, and maple syrup are delicious examples of liquid matter.

*Look at these three examples. Each picture shows water in a different state of matter. Can you tell which one is a solid, a liquid, or a gas?*

# Talking about matter

States of matter have different **properties**. Properties are ways to tell how something looks, feels, smells, or tastes. Properties are the qualities, or traits, that matter has.

*Liquid is matter that moves or flows easily. It can be poured from one container to another. The shape of a liquid changes to the same shape as its container.*

*When a liquid such as water is poured into a new container, the water's shape changes, but the amount of liquid stays the same.*

A solid is matter that does not change shape when it is moved from one container to another.

Gas is matter that is all around but cannot be seen. A gas will take the shape of the container it is in. A gas can also expand, or spread out, to completely fill the space in the container.

A solid, such as a book, always has the same shape and contains the same amount of material.

Inside a balloon, a gas such as air will take the same shape as the balloon. The gas expands to fill the whole space inside.

# A tall glass of matter

Did you drink a glass of matter today?
If you drank water, milk, or another
liquid, then the answer is yes!
Liquid is matter that flows.
This means you can pour it.

*This girl pours milk on her cereal. Milk is a liquid.*

## No shape of its own

A liquid does not have its own shape. A liquid takes the shape of the container holding it. This is why the same amount of liquid looks different in a tall, thin glass than in a short, wide glass.

**What do you think?**

*These glasses contain the same amount of juice. Why does one glass look as though it has more juice than the other?*

9

# Measuring liquid

A liquid takes up space. We measure liquid by **volume**. Volume tells us how much space a liquid takes up. When a liquid is poured from one container into another container, its shape changes but its volume stays the same.

*One property of liquid is how easily it can flow. Different types of liquids move at different speeds. Thin, slippery liquids such as water pour quickly at **room temperature**. Thick, sticky liquids such as honey pour much more slowly.*

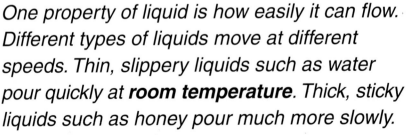

# What do you think?

## On your mark, get set, POUR!

*Pour one tablespoon of water, olive oil, and honey onto three separate spoons. With the help of two friends, pour each liquid from the spoons into a bowl at the same time. Which liquid reaches the bottom of the bowl first? Which one wins the race?*

*Both of these containers hold the same amount, or volume, of liquid.*

*We use a measuring cup to measure the volume of liquid.*

# Changing states

It is possible for matter to change from one state to another. **Physical changes** are changes in how an object looks. Physical changes happen when you add or take away heat energy from matter. Matter changes states when its temperature is changed. After being changed to a different state, some types of matter, such as water, can even be changed back to their first state.

Water is matter that can change easily from ice (a solid) to water (a liquid) to water **vapor** or steam (a gas). Water looks different in each of these states, but it is still always water.

**What do you think?**

*How many changes of state can you see when an adult heats ice cubes in a pot on the stove?*

# F-f-f-freezing!

Even though we cannot see them, the particles in a liquid are always moving. Liquid particles need energy to keep moving. Heat is a type of energy that makes particles move in a liquid.

To cool a liquid, we take heat away. The less energy particles get, the less they move. The particles come closer together. A liquid changes into a solid when enough heat energy has been taken away. This is called freezing. The temperature at which a liquid becomes a solid is called its **freezing point**. Different liquids have different freezing points.

# What do you think?

Water turns from a liquid into solid ice at 32 degrees Fahrenheit (0 degrees Celsius). What is the freezing point of water? (Hint: The answer is right here on this page!)

# Evaporation

The particles in a liquid are always moving. When more heat energy is added to a liquid, the particles have more energy and move even more. With enough heat energy, a liquid can change into a gas or vapor state. Vapor is an invisible gas. This change of state is called **evaporation**.

## Boiling water

Water boils at 212 degrees Fahrenheit (100 degrees Celsius). At this temperature, the water particles have so much energy they bounce into the air and create a cloud of steam. The steam is the boiling water evaporating, or changing from a liquid to a vapor.

**What do you think?**

*Yesterday there was a rain puddle on the sidewalk. Today it is gone. What made the puddle disappear?*

# Melting

Have you ever had a juice pop outside on a hot, sunny day? Most likely, after a few minutes, liquid from the juice pop dripped onto your fingers or the pavement. The heat from the sun changed the juice pop from a solid into a liquid. This change of state is called melting.

Many solids melt, or change from a solid to a liquid, when heat is added to them. The temperature at which a solid changes to a liquid is called its **melting point**. Solid water, or ice, changes to a liquid at 32 degrees Fahrenheit (0 degrees Celsius). Different types of matter have different melting points.

## What do you think?

*Put a hard piece of butter on a warm piece of toast. The butter begins to melt. Why do you think this happens?*

# Deliciously cool change of state

Here is a project in which you can make your own change of state and a tasty treat at the same time!

## What you will need:

2 cups (480 ml) fruit juice (apple, orange, grape, cranberry are a few suggestions)

4 small paper cups

4 craft sticks or small spoons

a freezer

# What to do:

1 Measure and pour ½ cup of fruit juice (120 ml) into each paper cup.

2 Place the cups on top of a flat pan and place it in the freezer.

3 After about 25 minutes, put the craft sticks in the middle of the fruit juice in the cups. Place the tray back in the freezer.

4 Wait about 2 hours. Your juice pops should be ready to eat!

# Using liquids

Liquids are useful because they can change their shape. Different types of liquids have different properties, which make them useful for certain jobs.

*Some liquids are used to make objects slide easier. Oil is used in car motors to make moving parts move more smoothly.*

*One type of paint is a mix of water and solid material. The liquid makes the paint easy to spread. The liquid then evaporates and leaves only the solid paint color on the object being painted.*

*Gasoline is not a gas. It is a liquid used as fuel to move cars.*

# Learning more

## Books

*Amazing Materials* (Amazing Science series)
by Sally Hewitt, Crabtree Publishing, 2008.

*Changing Materials* (Working with Materials series)
by Chris Oxlade, Crabtree Publishing, 2008.

## Websites

**www.linktolearning.com/grade2science.htm**
A list of science websites that help explain the properties
of solids and liquids.

**http://fossweb.com/modulesK-2/SolidsandLiquids/index.html**
Use the virtual oven or freezer on this website to change
a liquid into a solid or a solid into a liquid.

**www.harcourtschool.com/activity/states_of_matter**
Find out how particles in a solid, a liquid, or a gas behave
under a virtual microscope on this website.

**http://e-learningforkids.org/Courses/EN/S0602/index.html**
Mr. Beaker explains the three main states of matter, and how
and why they change, on this fun and interactive website.

# Glossary

**Note:** Some boldfaced words are defined where they appear in the book.

**evaporation** [ih-vap-uh-REY-shuhn] *noun* The change of state that happens when a liquid changes into a gas or vapor

**freezing point** [FREE-zing POYNT] *noun* The temperature at which a liquid changes into a solid

**melting point** [MEL-ting POYNT] *noun* The temperature at which a solid changes into a liquid

**physical change** [FIZ-i-kel CHAYNJ] *adjective and noun* A change in the way matter looks

**property** [PROP-er-tee] *noun* A special quality or attribute that a type of matter has

**room temperature** [RUME TEMP-er-a-chur] *adjective* Something that is the same temperature as the room it is in

**vapor** [VAY-per] *noun* Matter in a gas state

*A noun is a person, place, or thing. An adjective is a word that tells you what something is like.*

# Index

24